Wilderness
Ontario

Wilderness Ontario

GARY AND JOANIE MCGUFFIN

The BOSTON MILLS PRESS

A BOSTON MILLS PRESS BOOK

Published by Boston Mills Press, 2007
132 Main Street, Erin, Ontario N0B 1T0
Tel: 519-833-2407 Fax: 519-833-2195

In Canada:
Distributed by Firefly Books Ltd.
66 Leek Crescent
Richmond Hill, Ontario, Canada L4B 1H1

In the United States:
Distributed by Firefly Books (U.S.) Inc.
P.O. Box 1338, Ellicott Station
Buffalo, New York 14205

The publisher gratefully acknowledges for the financial support of our publishing program the Canada Council, the Ontario Arts Council, and the Government of Canada through the Book Publishing Industry Development Program (BPIDP).

Library and Archives Canada Cataloguing in Publication

McGuffin, Gary, 1959-
Wilderness Ontario / Gary and Joanie McGuffin.

ISBN 978-1-55046-504-4

1. Wilderness areas — Ontario — Pictorial works.
2. Ontario — Pictorial works. I. McGuffin, Joanie, 1960– II. Title.

FC3062.M33 2007 917.130022'2 C2007-901747-9

Publisher Cataloging-in-Publication Data (U.S.)

McGuffin, Gary, 1959-
Wilderness Ontario / Gary and Joanie McGuffin.

[240] p. : col. photos. ; cm.
Includes index.
Summary: A collection of images of wilderness Ontario, Canada, taken during two decades of travel to every corner of the province.

ISBN-13: 978-1-55046-504-4
ISBN-10: 1-55046-504-X

1. Wilderness areas — Ontario — History — 20th century — Pictorial works.
2. Ontario — History — 20th century — Pictorial works. I. McGuffin, Joanie, 1960– II. Title.

333.95160971 dc22 QH77.C2.M347 2007

FACING PAGE:
Near Gids Harbour in Pukaskwa, one of Canada's most beautiful national parks, are 1878 square kilometres (725 square miles) of Canadian Shield and boreal forest that include some of the grandest shoreline in the world. The colours of the landscape are vivid and the view of the sunsets just perfect.

Design by Gillian Stead

Printed in China

For Sila

May you always find a sense of belonging whenever you are in the wilds of Ontario.

INTRODUCTION

Draw a freehand map of Ontario, and I almost guarantee that you will not show enough distance north to south. This province is a vast and varied landscape, from island-studded Lake of the Woods to the great Ottawa River, and from Lake Erie's Point Pelee north to the Black Duck River on Hudson Bay.

Gary and I experienced "wilderness Ontario" from an early age. The valleys of the upper Thames and the upper Don, in our respective school-year homes of London and Thornhill, were our wild oases, places where we could find refuge in nature. Thirty-five years ago, when we were children, our parents gave us the freedom to explore these places. Nature was much closer at hand then, even in proximity to Canada's large urban centres. We grew up relishing all four seasons, but we lived with a passion for summer months spent in cottages on Temagami's Rabbit Lake and Muskoka's Lake Joseph. In these backwoods, we roamed, on foot and by canoe, learning about native animals, plants and trees, and honing our wilderness skills. Most especially, our mutual fascination for exploring wild places had its roots in the immense number of navigable lakes and rivers.

Part of our route on our first long canoe voyage, from the Gulf of St. Lawrence to the Beaufort Sea, took us across Ontario, through wilderness places both familiar and long dreamed of. Through the simple act of canoeing, we found ourselves becoming part of everything these waterways had ever known. At ancient flint-knapping sites, stone tent rings, and certain sand-beach campsites, we found stone spear points and pottery shards that still bore marks of human handling. These implements seemed to hold the dreams and aspirations of their makers, people who lived as far back as 11,000 years ago.

At sunset, a path of smoke from a raging forest fire in the Steel River valley casts an eerie red glow over our campsite in Morn Harbour.

The photographs in this book were all taken on our wilderness journeys, in all four seasons and by many different modes of self-propelled travel. It is during times like these that we feel most in balance: physically fit, emotionally fulfilled, intellectually challenged by weather, water and navigation conditions, and spiritually close to all that sustains our lives.

The landscape is transformed markedly by each distinct season. As artists, we no doubt benefit from living in a place with four separate seasons. As the Earth's relation to the sun changes through the days and the seasons, so do the intensity, quality and colours of light. Skies, clouds and storms distinctive to the spring, summer, fall and winter form rhythms that we intuitively count on, nature's clock being more imbedded in our psyche than clock time. Using various methods of self-propelled travel, we are able to cover the same ground in all seasons. At the very same place where we pick blueberries and swim on hot July afternoons, we also set up our canvas tent for winter camping on -30-degree Celsius nights in January. Through this book, we'd like to share with you our experiences coastal kayaking on Georgian Bay beneath Killarney's La Cloche range, canoeing the shores of Lake Nipigon, snowshoe-trekking on Quetico's frozen lakes, dogsledding Temagami's Nastawgan, and exploring our own backyard along Lake Superior's eastern shore, through all seasons. We have travelled together, just the two of us, as well as with friends, with our dog and in recent years with our daughter. Encounters with white pelicans, black bears, bald eagles, caribou, moose, timberwolves and otters have melded into our larger life experience and become, to us, what we think of as "home."

North of Sudbury, Ojibwa artists and shamans of long ago used this rock wall rising from the depths of Scotia Lake's blue waters as a painter's canvas.

What intrigues us most is that just by getting out in the wilderness, our senses become sharper. Because the sensory experiences of nature were imprinted upon us early in life, each new season awakens memories that sweep us back to childhood along a timeline marked with wilderness journeys. Summer is found in the taste of fish freshly caught and raspberries picked. Autumn is in the smell of fallen maple leaves as we shuffle through a blaze of colour during a woodland hike. Winter is the feel of each tingling breath and in the small white clouds we expel into the frigid air as we skate the length of a frozen lake beneath the pulsating northern lights. But in this part of Canada, it is spring where the sensation of the life force is most keenly felt, as the silence of winter gives way to the dawn chorus of birds, the nightly frog song and the sound of melting, dripping, rushing water. The black-and-white world suddenly bursts with colour in tiny flowers, young birds, the greening forest, all of it reflected in water and sky. Sweet-smelling violets, arbutus, and warm earth are deeply inhaled after the seemingly scentless winter months.

If we can absorb these aspects of the seasons in Ontario's wilderness by experiencing them first-hand, most especially with our children, we can perhaps better connect with all living things. We do not need to know the names of each plant and bird. We need only stop and listen, feel, smell, taste and see with a renewed sense of wonder. Imagine that each moment is both your first and your last. The warmth of the spring sunshine and the rush of clean, fresh water should remind us of that which makes our existence possible.

Ontario's wilderness is vast, yet it is also nearer than we think. We need only slow down and make it part of our lives.

A lone pine seedling has taken hold in a crevasse on the white granite of Argo Lake in Quetico Provincial Park. One wonders at the tenacity of a seed to germinate in this seemingly hostile environment and, furthermore, to mature into a white pine standing sentinel for several centuries to come.

Haentschel Lake is at the top of the watershed between the Sturgeon and Wanapitei rivers. Portage trails leading east and west out of the lake require some hard slogging through overgrown and boggy trails. Such effort is well worth it for the assurance of a remote and pristine campsite.

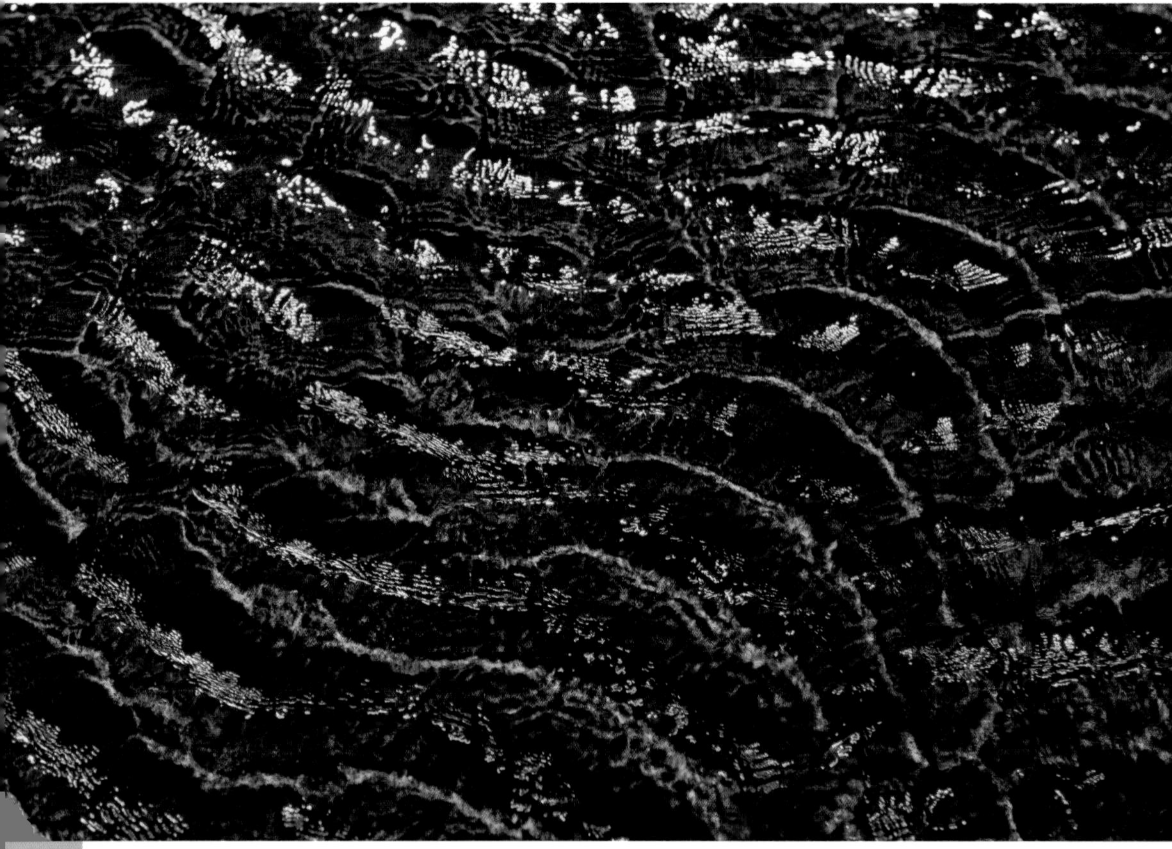

Wave patterns at the mouth of the Imogene River
capture both the reflected blue of sky and the gold of brown-sugar sand.

We meet an elder from Pic River First Nation who provides us with a map containing original Ojibwa place names along the Pukaskwa coast. Pukaskwa is Bukaszhaawe, pronounced Puk-shay-wa and meaning "the cleaning of fish." To us, Pukaskwa is bright, clear water where the shadow of your canoe flies beneath you like the shadow of a large bird.

Small chanterelles emerging through the moist sphagnum moss of Temagami's White Bear old-growth forest.

Afternoon light on an island on Baird Lake in northwestern Ontario. Maidenhair ferns grow upon the steeper hillside beneath the young stand of red pine.

Ancient rock formations and huge rolling headlands with sheer cliffs and bald summits characterize the Lake Superior coast south to Cascade Falls. On our way to this place, the most remote on the entire Great Lakes coastline, we pass the White Gravel, White Spruce, and Swallow rivers. The rolling, rugged terrain is cut through with major ruptures or fault valleys, the Cascade River being one of them.

Kneeling on padded saddles in the centre of our solo canoes, we feel like rodeo riders on bucking broncos as we descend through the Dog River's shadowy gorges. Above the din of the water's roar come the clear-noted warble of winter wrens, a trill that fills the whole forest with springtime.

Following a cool, moonlit night amongst Georgian Bay's Thirty Thousand Islands, a thick fog dissipates with the rising sun.

Waves washing against the shore at Imogene Bay.

Glacial erratics. Montreal River Harbour, Lake Superior.

Lake Superior's wave-tumbled, colourful, perfectly smooth rocks.

Veins of quartz sweep across the glacier-scoured, metamorphic rocks on Elm Tree Island. Georgian Bay's rock formations are an attraction for the geologist in all of us.

White cedar growing on the banks provides a cool, shaded habitat for many forest dwellers along the Darkwater River.

On a month-long circumnavigation of Lake Nipigon,
we stop near the mouth of the Whitesand River for lunch and a swim.

Roasting marshmallows and telling stories as we relax by the campfire, hypnotized by the dancing flames at the end of a summer day, is a memorable part of our family's northern Ontario adventures. All along the northern and eastern shores of Lake Superior, there are beautiful, secluded sand coves accessible to those who travel self-propelled by kayak and canoe.

North Bay, Lake Nipigon.

Portaging around Aubrey Falls on the Mississagi River.

Birchbark and sand create a miniature scene of spruce forest and hills. Taking time to view the Earth from different perspectives, such as those a child experiences down low to the ground, allows us to see familiar things in a fresh, new way.

Water-sculpted rock on the Dog River.

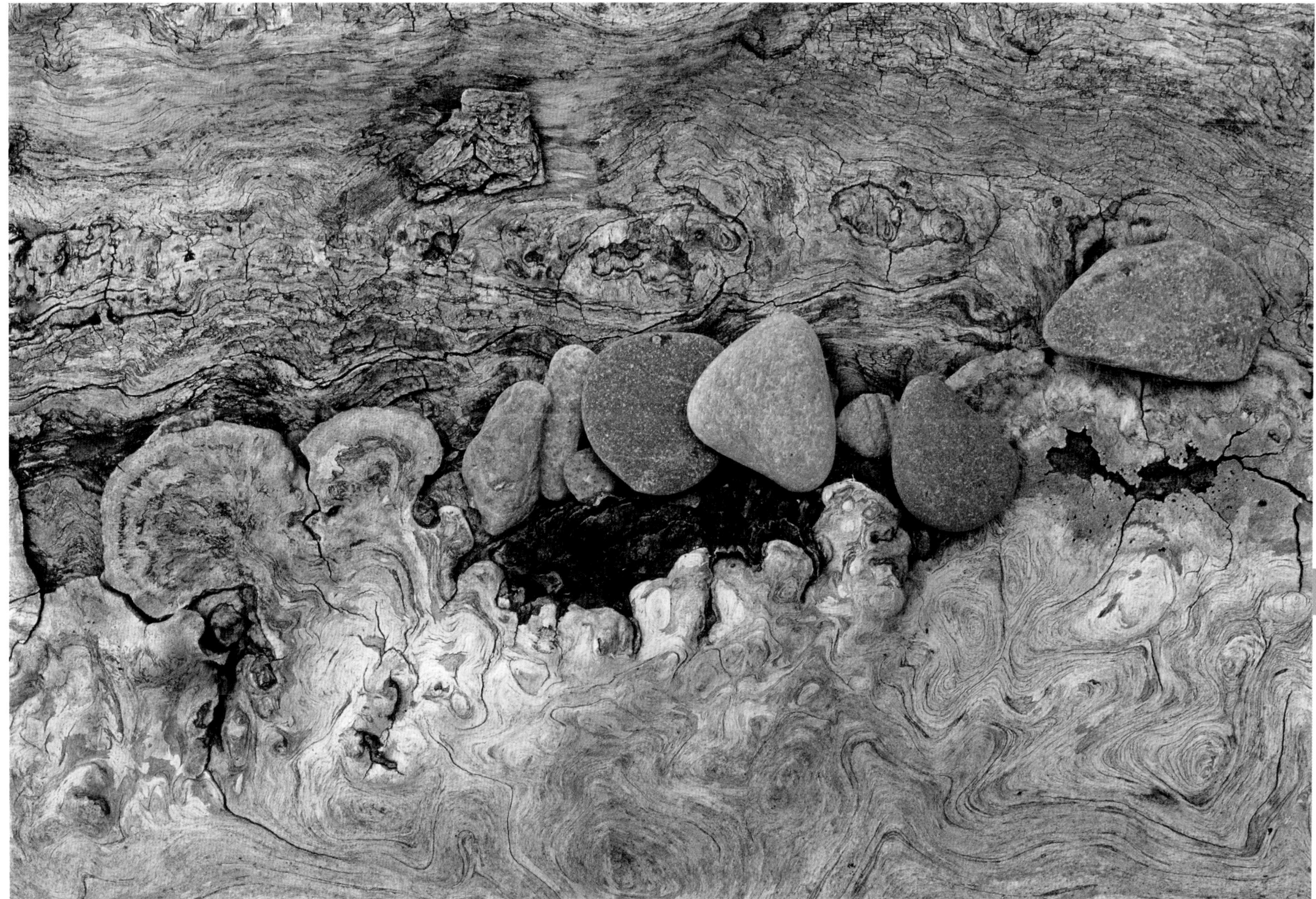

Waves have tossed a handful of small, flat stones ashore to rest on a piece of gnarly driftwood near the Dog River.

Clipping the handle to a band on our daughter's waist ensures that she can freely fly the parabolic kite without fear of losing it. Near the French River on Georgian Bay, the smooth, flat rocks are a perfect place to catch the wind.

Dedicated sunrise and sunset watchers know the weather proverb "Red sky in morning, sailors take warning; red sky at night, sailors delight." Gord Lake in the Algoma highlands.

Sugar maples shed their fall bounty of colourful leaves into the streams and onto the floor of the Great Lakes–St. Lawrence forest south of the boreal in a thick leaf mat that prevents seedlings other than maples from thriving. Hence, the familiar autumn blaze of gold and red forest canopy in many places in wilderness Ontario.

Overlooking Paradise Island's reefs, red rock and raised beaches on the south side of St. Ignace Island, Lake Superior.

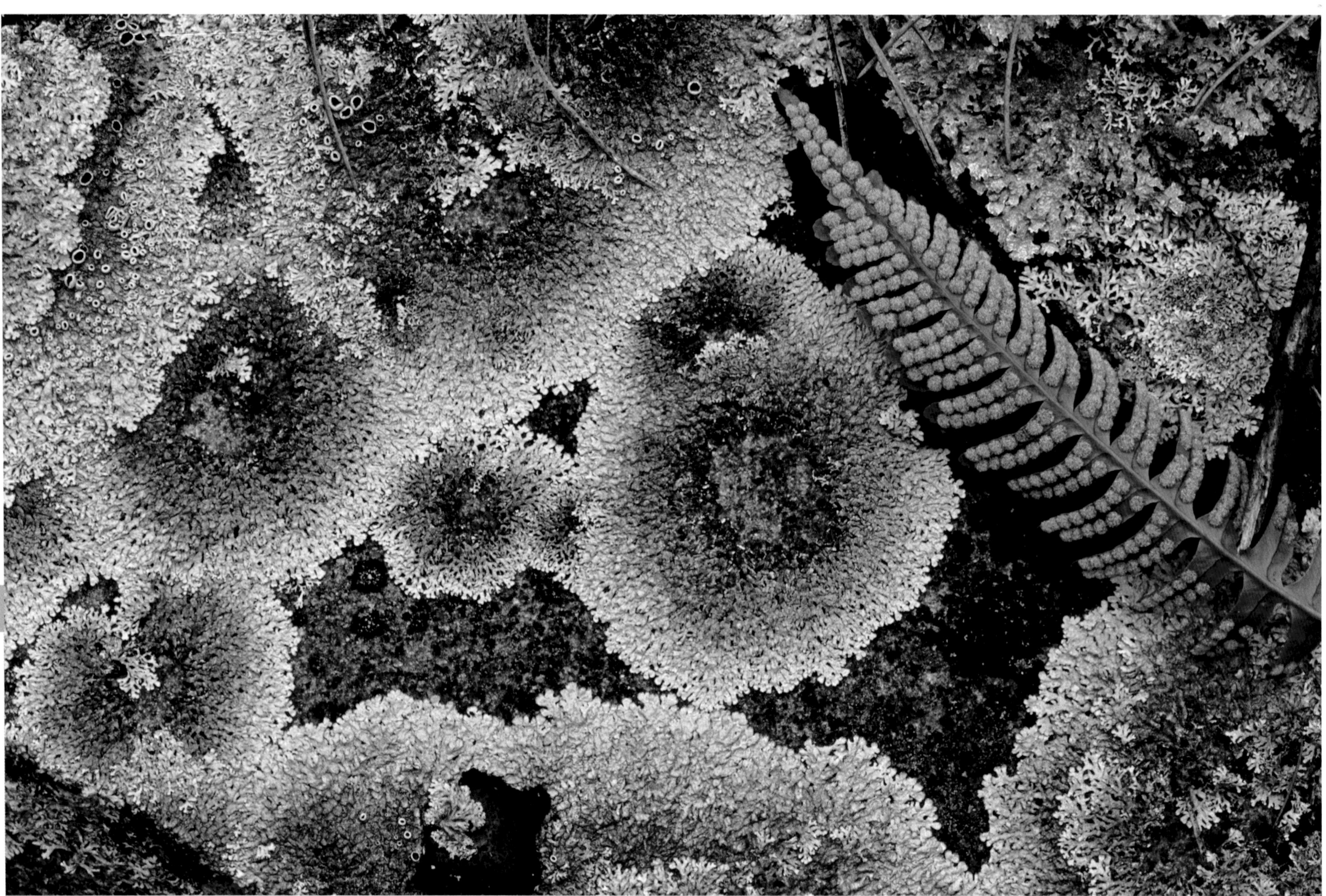

A fertile fern frond lies on the map lichen spreading over granite rock. In dry weather, this lichen is brittle and crumbles underfoot, but in the rain, it absorbs moisture, becoming leathery and very slippery to walk over.

Group of Seven painter Lawren Harris immortalized Pic Island in his magnificent canvas painted in 1924.
The exaggerated height of the island hills rising from a pool of white light most certainly enhances the enchantment this place already radiates.

Among the shoreline boulders near the Montreal River mouth, there are some whose distinctive smooth shapes catch our eye, raising the question as to why they are so different from the rest.

A tiny balsam flourishes in the shelter of a driftwood knot from which a tree branch once grew.

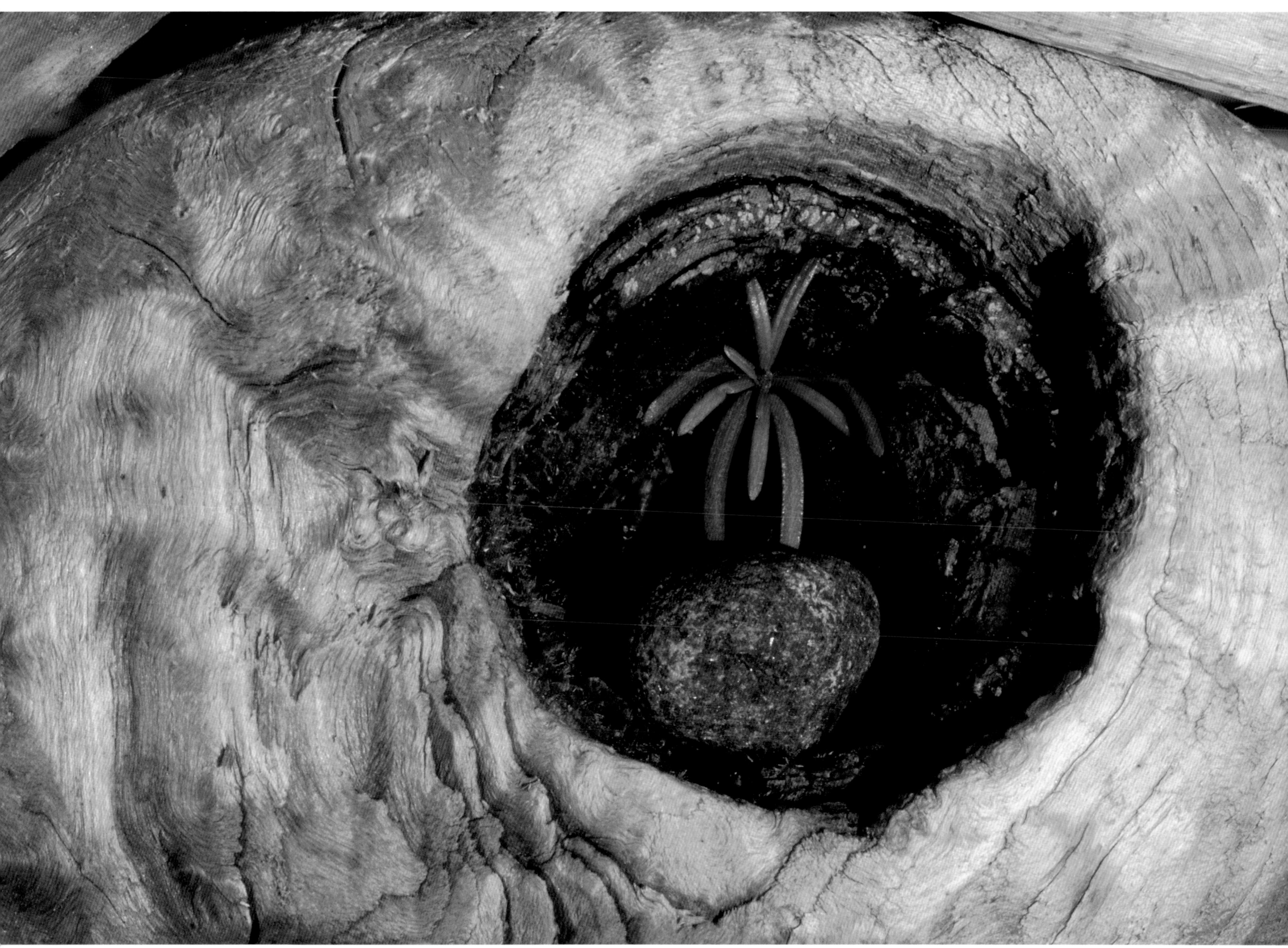

Silver Island, south of Philip Edward Island, near Killarney.

The smooth granite of Fox Harbour's Benjamin Islands in the North Channel of Lake Huron reflects the fiery glow of an autumn sunset.

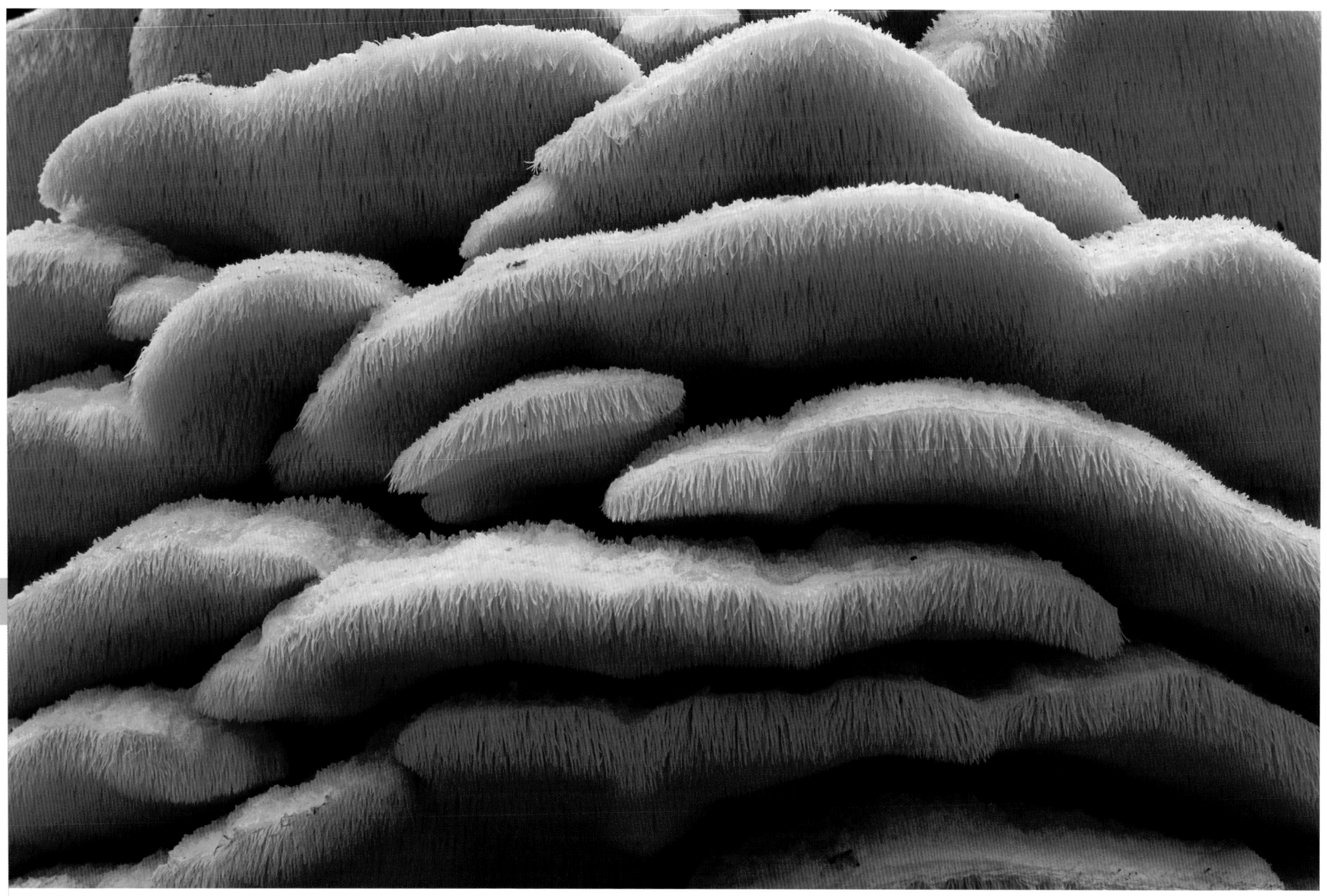

Large, overlapping, shelf-like mushrooms called Northern Tooth grow high up on living sugar maples. Batchawana Bay.

Ridges of white pine pierce the sea of early morning mist in the Algoma highlands.
These green islands fill the great ocean of air with the oxygen all animals need to survive.

This image of wave-washed granite, taken at sunrise on the shore of Martin Island, seems to capture the four elements of life: earth, water, fire and air.

Year round, white quartzite gives La Cloche range near Killarney its characteristic snow-capped-mountain look.
These old mountains provide some of wilderness Ontario's loveliest hiking, and the islands are a great coastal paddling destination.

The view from atop Ontario's highest vertical cliffs in Sleeping Giant Provincial Park shows Tee Harbour and the islands of Lake Superior to distant Isle Royale. Let your imagination take you back thirteen thousand years to when the Great Lakes basin was still filled with the last of the Wisconsin glacial ice. Where we stand on these 244-metre (800-foot) cliffs, the waters of a newly forming lake shoreline would just be emerging. The forested land was an open tundra of swaying grasses, dwarf birch and scrub willow, alive with roaming inhabitants, including the now extinct woolly mammoth.

In various places on shoreline cliffs and rock outcrops across the Canadian Shield, red ochre pictographs have withstood centuries of weathering. Misshepezhieu, the great lynx and god of the waters, is portrayed vividly on the stone canvas rising from Darkwater Lake in Quetico. The lynx's tail lies in the water beneath the canoes, and when this serpent-like appendage thrashes the lake, stormy seas ensue. Passing travellers have long shown their respect by leaving offerings of tobacco.

The Nipigon's fine sand floats on water, casting shadows on the river bottom the same way one sees, from a seaplane travelling into a remote lake, the shadows of cumulous clouds floating over the land.

Sunrise on Scarecrow Lake, below Ontario's highest point of land, Ishpatina Ridge.

On a cool September morning, these clouds form bands over the islands south of Killarney Provincial Park.

Inner Barn Island emerges from the early morning fog over Lake Nipigon's Wabinosh Bay.

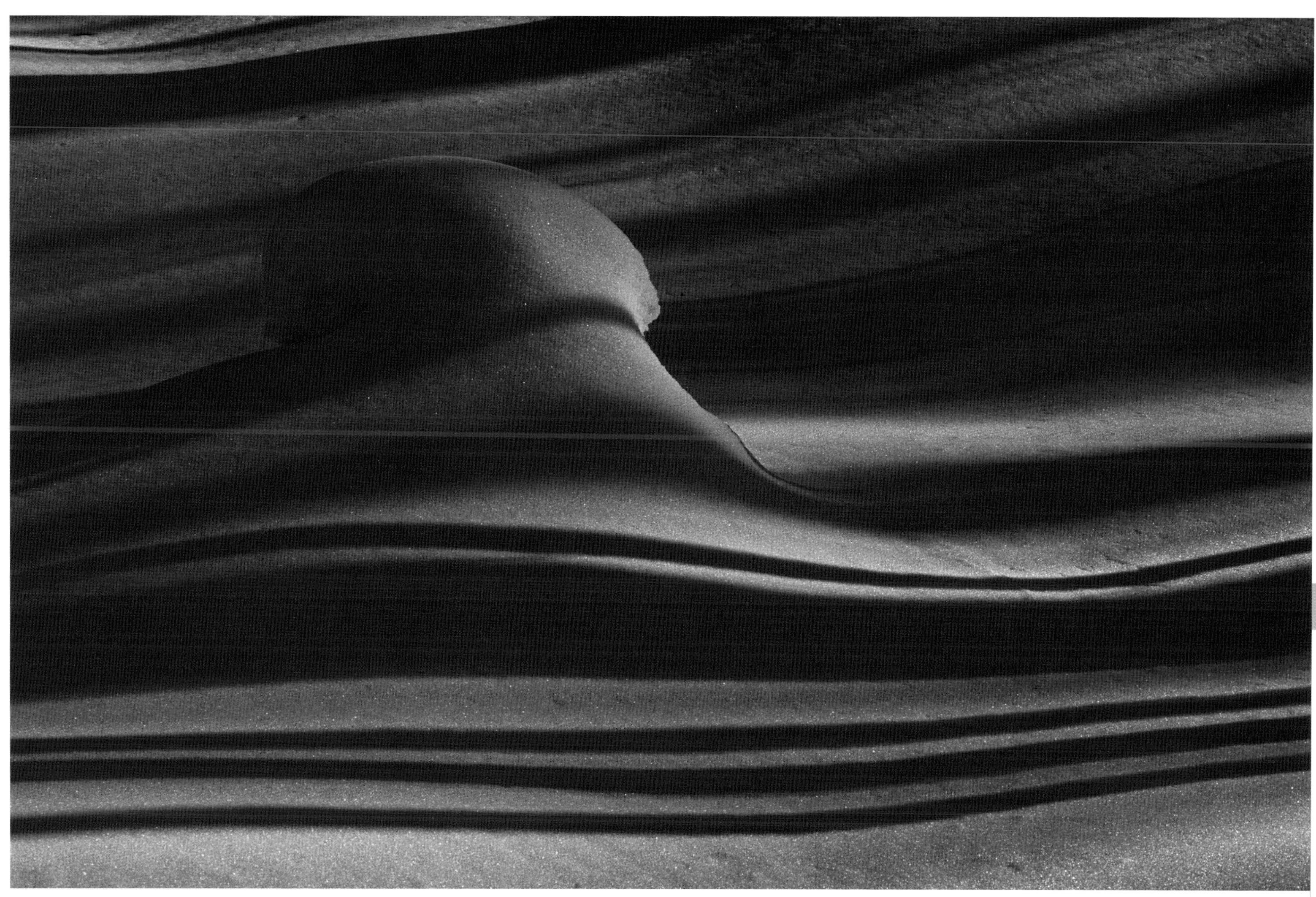

On a late January afternoon, hardwoods cast long shadows across the deep powder snow near the summit of Batchawana Mountain.

This woodland caribou symbolizes the very habitat it calls home. Roaming the boreal forest from the north shore of Lake Superior to James Bay, these caribou have adapted as nomadic herd animals, dependent on the old-growth lichens that sustain them through the winters of deep snows and intense cold. Their reliance on large areas of old-growth boreal forest, undisturbed by humans, has made them iconic creatures in the effort to protect the greatest terrestrial ecosystem on Earth.

Close-up of red pine bark on Sturgeon Lake, northwestern Ontario.

I spend an afternoon with our young daughter playing in these weather-sculpted rocks on western Fox Island near Killarney. Our favourite game is taking a bucket of water and pouring it slowly from the top so that it fills one bowl and then spills over into each successive bowl until a stream eventually reaches the lake.

As night falls, we sit on the rocks of Foster Island admiring the reflecting pools and distant Pic Island, waiting for the moment when darkness allows us to see the stars. Contemplating the night sky is not so much about "what is out there" as it is about appreciating the gift of being human and the luck of living on this abundant planet Earth.

Most of our views of black bears have been brief glimpses as we approach them, silently drifting along the shore in our canoe. During these encounters, the bears are unaware of our presence, busy foraging for insect larvae near the water's edge. Once we are recognizable, the first bear pauses briefly before bounding off into the woods with amazing speed and grace. Contrary to the false image of a ravenous carnivore, the black bear's main foods are fruits, nuts and insects. It is extraordinary that such a large animal can build up its fat reserves on this diet and sustain itself during winter hibernation.

Water patterns on the North Wind River, Lake Nipigon.

Eastern white pine can live five hundred years and attain a height of 50 metres (165 feet), given optimum growing conditions. This magnificent feathery-limbed species is Ontario's official tree.

Waves sculpting an ever-changing pattern on the beach at Oiseau Bay.

The stretch of Great Lakes coastline that lies between Pukaskwa National Park and Lake Superior Provincial Park, west of the Michipicoten River, is a landscape whose beauty is second to none.

Driftwood detail.

We take refuge in Bottle Cove after a thick, soupy fog and rising wind catches us unawares. We have been grateful on more than one occasion for the protection this place offers.

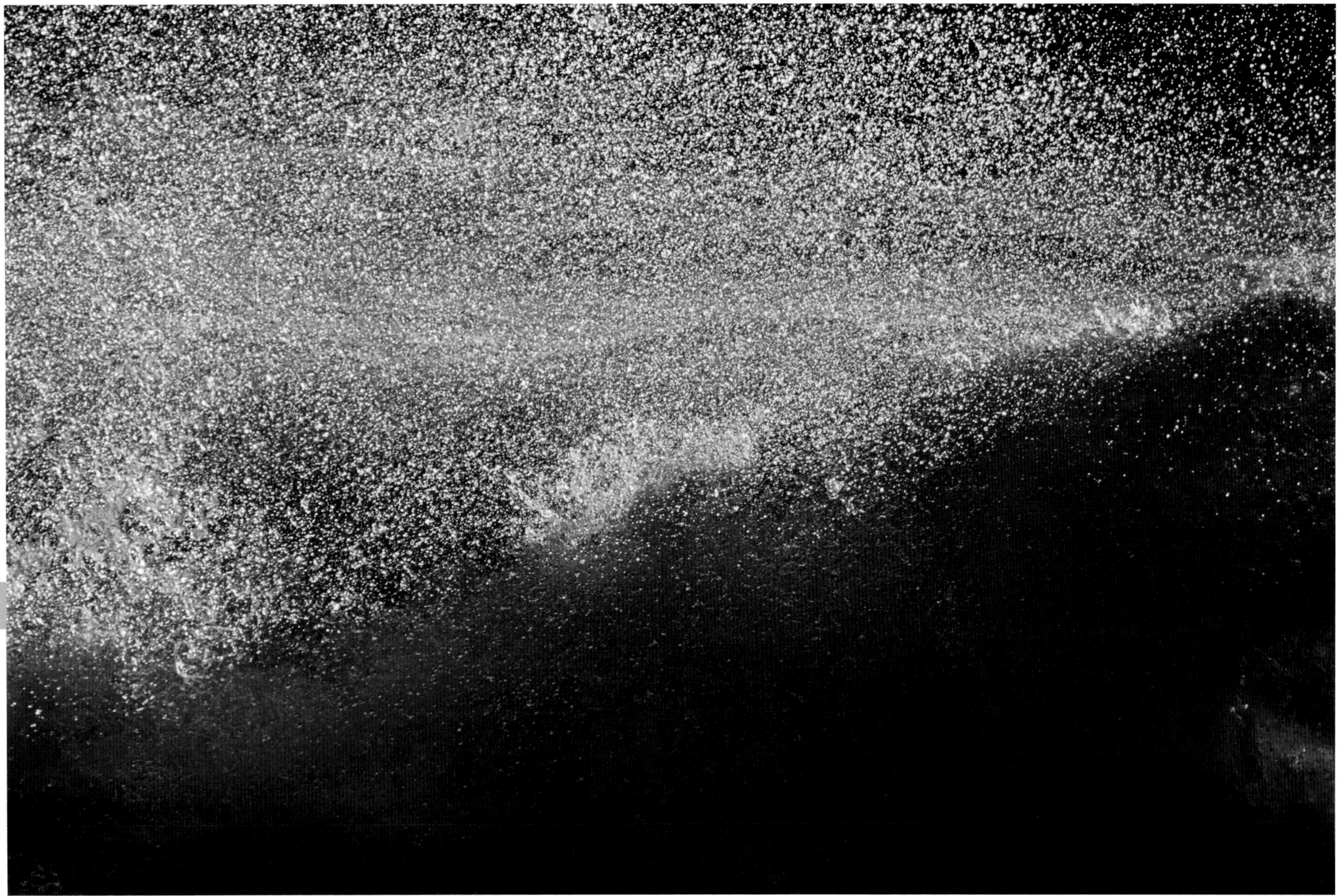

Even from an early age, we can both remember liking big waves. The way they thunder in, booming and throwing spray, is a spine-tingling experience that we have shared with our daughter on many occasions, from the time she was a baby.

Along the Agawa River, the first golden and red hints of autumn appear in the white pine, birch and sugar maple. This canoe adventure begins with a ride on the Algoma Central Railway wilderness train. We unload our canoes from the baggage car in the steep-walled Agawa Canyon and then head downstream to Lake Superior.

These patterns were left on a poplar tree by a porcupine gnawing at the trunk. These prickly mammals also adore the salty taste of anything touched by human hands. Once we awoke to find our friend's leather pack straps completely devoured. Nothing was left but a trail of telltale pigeon-toed paw prints leading back to the woods.

Paddling in from Michipicoten Bay, we discover this sun-filled pool of white foam lying at the base of a waterfall.
The river is stained as dark as strong tea by the tannins leaching into it from the exposed, entwined tree roots that grow along its banks.

Intrusions of black lava snake through the metamorphic rocks near Wreck Island on Georgian Bay.

The hike into the White River basin from Pukaskwa National Park headquarters at Hattie Cove can be a beautiful day trip or the beginning of a week-long trek on the Coastal Trail. The big drop below this gorge is Chigamiwinigum Falls, which means "first falls up from the lake."

Only human beings see Curtain Falls, situated between Quetico Provincial Park and the Boundary Waters canoeing area, as the international border between Canada and the United States. For all other life forms, there is no *fence*, only flowing water connecting one lake to another and eventually to the salty sea. It is a short whitewater run of two to three days with the kind of spectacular scenery made famous by Canada's Group of Seven artists.

In the world of a little waterfall deep within the Algoma highlands, a pool swirling with fallen leaves becomes a magical fairyland. If we examine the small, inconspicuous places in nature, we will always find something new and intriguing. Nature is never dull.

The first hint of sunrise peeks through Temagami's ancient forest. Marina Lake.

White pine forest along the Mississagi River.

Looking down the great sweep of beach at Imogene Cove. At the beach's east end, on the other side of Imogene Creek, lie the remains of a 1920s winter logging camp, the Pukaskwa Depot.

Birch on the Matabitchuan River. White (or paper) birch is a highly valuable medicinal and food source for many songbirds and mammals. Aboriginal people also used the bark beneath the outer birch paper in making baskets, dishes, wigwams and canoes.

Autumn reflection in the Great Lakes–St. Lawrence forest.

Offshore reef at Campbell Point near Hattie Cove.

Returning from Montreal Island before the storm.

Fireweed thriving along the banks of the Pic River.

At twilight, the silver path of a full moon glitters softly across the waters off Desjardin Point, Georgian Bay.

During a three-month journey, while exploring and mapping a route across Northern Ontario that linked together the ancient forests of red and white pine, we discovered the historical significance of the Amable du Fond River as a link between the north end of Algonquin Provincial Park and the Ottawa Valley. This whitewater river with its spectacular gorges was both a surprise and a highlight along the Ancient Forest Water Trail.

An ice-cold spring cascades down the moss and spills out onto the beach near Tee Harbour.

Introducing young children in a real hands-on way to the wonders of nature fosters an instinct for the awe-inspiring beauty to be found every day in each of our lives. It is a precious gift that brings lifelong pleasure.

From early spring to late fall, Ontario's forests and waterways are filled with an ever-changing array of scents, from the woodland's fragrant arbutus and violets to the lakes where sweet, white water lilies grow.

This small, patterned tiger moth appeared like a bright jewel on the long beach at North Bay, Lake Nipigon. The stripes warn predators not to eat this insect as it is filled with bad-tasting chemicals. At night, these moths make ultrasonic sounds to warn their main predators, the bats, that they are a bad-tasting dinner.

In a bog along a portage trail west of the Spanish River that runs between a series of pretty little lakes called Dennie, Gilden, Sinaminda, Landry and Dusty, we came across pitcher plants. These insectivores obtain their nutrients by attracting insects with their red colour and then trapping them in their leaf tubes. The insects dissolve and the plants consume them.

Pitching a canvas tent and using a small woodstove for heat make the long, cold, dark nights on a winter camping trip enjoyable.

South of Anima Nipissing, we travelled with a team of Canadian Inuit dogs, arguably the hardiest of sled-dog breeds for journeys of more than one day. For years we have explored the *nastawgan*, the traditional winter and summer routes of Temagami.

Autumn on Taylor Creek in the Algoma highlands.

Quetico Provincial Park, located 200 kilometres (125 miles) west of Thunder Bay on the Canada-US border, is famous for its extensive network of canoe routes, which meander through a pristine wilderness, free of motorized boats and vehicles.

The Great Lakes hold the largest volume of freshwater on the planet, and Lake Superior is the greatest expanse of this precious substance.

A week-long whitewater canoe trip on the Pukaskwa River is followed by 100 kilometres (60 miles) of flatwater canoeing along the wonderfully isolated shoreline to reach the community of Michipicoten Harbour.

Adventures into nature were part of our upbringing. We are now passing along the experience of making exciting and unexpected discoveries in all seasons, through journeying together as a family.

Sunrise near the mouth of the Kopka River, Lake Nipigon.

Lady Evelyn River above Centre Falls, Temagami.

Storm clouds gather at the mouth of Imogene River, Lake Superior.

Grant Point, Eight Mile Island.

Looking west from Eight Mile Island toward Shakespeare Island on Lake Nipigon.

Ontario is a vast province stretching from the Carolinian forest of Point Pelee on Lake Erie northwards to Polar Bear Provincial Park. It would surprise many people to know that these arctic mammals live in Ontario. They epitomize adaptation to a harsh and rigorous climate. Their thick fur keeps them warm, and they can swim for many hours in the freezing waters of Hudson Bay.

Loons nest on quiet lakes and bays. Their nests are built right next to the water because a loon's legs are set too far back on its body to walk on land. Both the male and female raise the young, which average two chicks per nest. A healthy lake with lots of live food such as minnows is necessary for the chicks' survival.

Centre Falls on the Lady Evelyn River, Temagami.

Greenstone, False Dog Harbour, Lake Superior.

Thessalon Point, North Channel of Lake Huron.

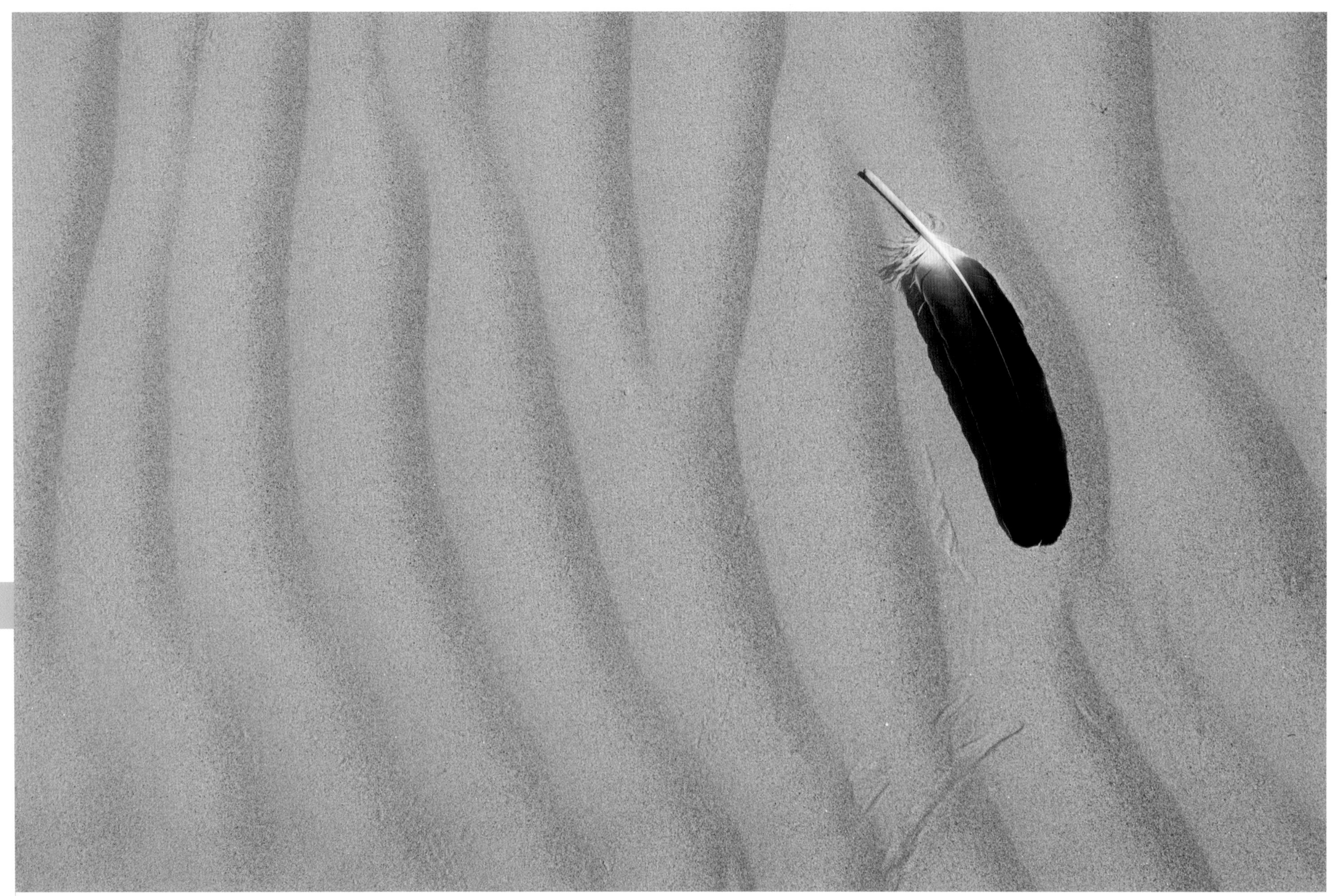

Two elements of our month-long journey paddling around Lake Nipigon: a bald eagle feather and sand. Not a day passed that we didn't see one of the lake's 125 nesting pairs.

With water levels low the summer we paddled around Nipigon, most of our campsites were on narrow beaches. Sandpipers were often probing the wet sand along the edge of these warm, shallow pools.

After a particularly windy crossing between Battle and Wilson islands, we are happy to take refuge in the tranquil bay behind the high hill of Quarry Island. When Lake Superior's surface is smooth like this, we always feel that euphoric sense of moving in three-dimensional space as if we were flying.

During the first half of the twentieth century, timber companies logged the boreal forest of Lake Superior's north shore for pulpwood and paper. The trees, cut in early winter, were floated down the rivers in spring and collected in bays by huge free-floating booms. A woody carpet of sunken logs collected on the lake bottom in places like McGreevy Harbour in the Slate Islands.

Sunset at Tugboat Channel, Gargantua,
Lake Superior Provincial Park.

The Cascade River in Pukaskwa National Park is one of more than two hundred rivers that flow into Lake Superior.

In the autumn, one of our favourite day trips is a hike along the varied terrain of the Orphan Lake trail, which meanders past the rapids and waterfalls of the Baldhead River and climbs to spectacular outlooks.

Autumn reflection in the Great Lakes–St. Lawrence forest.

When the last ice age retreated ten thousand years ago, the vegetation was subarctic. As the climate warmed, the Great Lakes–St. Lawrence forest eventually emerged with white pines dominating the forest crown. This wilderness of conifers and deciduous species once covered a vast area from the northern Appalachians to Lake Superior and from the Mississippi to the Atlantic coast.

Naonan Island, Lake Nipigon.

Impending storm over Batchawana Bay.

White water lilies.

McCrae Lake, just a portage east of Georgian Bay.

West Fox Island, North Channel.

Sunset reflection south of Henvey Inlet, Georgian Bay.

Wood lily, Makwa River.

On the shores of a narrow lake with a backdrop of precipitous cliffs, we rest while our friend, native elder Alex Mathias, explains that Chee-skon-abikong Saw-gi-hay-gun-ning, or "the lake at the place of the huge rock," was one of the most spiritually important sites in all of Temagami.

A mirror-calm morning at the mouth of the White River in Pukaskwa National Park.

FACING PAGE: Snowstorm over Batchawana Bay.

PREVIOUS PAGE: Smoothwater Lake, Temagami.

A speckling of fish-scale clouds foretell changing weather. Lance Lake in the Algoma highlands.

Beneath Lake Superior's Sleeping Giant, Tee Harbour, Lake Superior.

Early morning from the top of Maple Mountain, known by the Teme Augama Anishnabai as Chee-bay-jing, "the place where the spirits go."

On this dark evening on the West Aubinadong River, we pitch our tent on flat rock. The roar of the river cascades through dreams of our summer's voyage from Algonquin Provincial Park to Lake Superior. In early June we set off to establish a 1900-kilometre (1,180-mile) route linking Ontario's finest examples of ancient forest landscape. This was a route once travelled by Canada's early conservationist Archie Belaney, better known as Grey Owl. Back then the wilderness was largely roadless. Rivers, lakes and portages were the only pathways through cedar swamps, great pine forests and vast stands of hemlock, sugar maple and oak.

White pine needles are a good source of vitamin C and, when chewed, also serve as a mouth freshener. If brewed, they make an invigorating tea.

On a journey through the forest, your passage is as fleeting as the path carved by your canoe. Yet, in passing, every place writes a story on your heart. Owain Lake, Temagami.

Sunrise on Foster Island, Neys Provincial Park. This is a place of smooth, flat rocks, reflecting pools and sandy strands strewn with the tracks of caribou and timber wolf.

A forest “on fire” with the light of sunset, Becor Lake.

Sugar maples provide maple sap in spring, which can be boiled down to sweet maple syrup.

Come autumn, when chlorophyll production ceases and green sugar maple leaves lose their green, sweeping uplands blaze with the true colours of these hardwoods. A view from the Robertson Lake cliffs near Goulais Bay.

In the early summer, the white flowers of bunchberries are a common sight along the portage trails of the Great Lakes–St. Lawrence woodlands. Later they form bunches of bright red berries, a favourite food of grouse and deer.

Camped on the cobble beach beside Cascade Falls.

From our windbound campsite at False Dog Harbour, we can see Michipicoten Bay to the east. South winds blowing across a 322-kilometre (200-mile) fetch have built up heavy seas too rough to handle in our open canoes. Along this wild section of Lake Superior coast, there are headlands of greenstone interspersed with sandy coves.

The polished white quartzite of La Cloche range is one of Ontario's most spectacular geological features. Within Killarney Provincial Park, we have canoed the crystal-clear lakes and hiked the trails to these snow-white peaks. In autumn, we kayak out into these islands to the south.

Picking and eating wild blueberries is a highlight of a summer canoe trip. Biscotasi Lake.

Near McLean's Creek looking toward the Cat Islands in Schreiber Channel.

Storm front over the Namewaminikan River, Lake Nipigon.

Travelling in the protection of islands north of Pointe au Baril enables us to make progress despite days of constant wind in Georgian Bay's Thirty Thousand Islands. Waves tumbling over the many reefs in white streamers make us think of the many ships lost in watery graves, claimed by these treacherous waters.

Club moss, also known as ground pine, is neither a low-growing conifer nor a type of moss. These pretty evergreens with their dense, narrow single-veined leaves are most closely related to horsetails and ferns. Since their spores rarely germinate, they propagate by creeping along the ground. However, their spore powder is flammable and has historically been used in fireworks and for flash explosions in photography.

Flying the kite on a windbound day at Imogene Bay.

A solitary white pelican appeared out of the fog like a ghost ship. Wabinosh Bay, Lake Nipigon.

Near Killarney's La Cloche Mountains, this smooth Precambrian rock on West Fox Island was scraped clean by the glaciers ten millennia ago.

The sound of chattering rocks rolled around by the waves is as intriguing a sensation as the feel of one of them in your hands.

Pic Island on the distant horizon viewed from Pebble Beach at Marathon.

Twin flowers in full bloom on Battle Island.

Near the great throne of black basalt known as Nanabijou's Chair, this enchanted landscape is filled with strange promontories and islands sculpted out of the porous volcanic rock. It is easy to imagine why this place has always held deep spiritual significance for First Nations people.

Looking out at the Windigo Islands from the mouth of Kenna Creek, Lake Nipigon.

There is a harmonious feeling to an old-growth forest, where complex relationships exist between a seemingly endless variety of flowers, ferns, mosses, fungi, trees, insects, birds and mammals. Baird Lake, Quetico Provincial Park.

This cluster of Orange Earth Tongues is growing, characteristically, among mosses in rich humus.

Evenings in the Slate Islands are cool enough for a campfire made with small pieces of driftwood found along the shore.

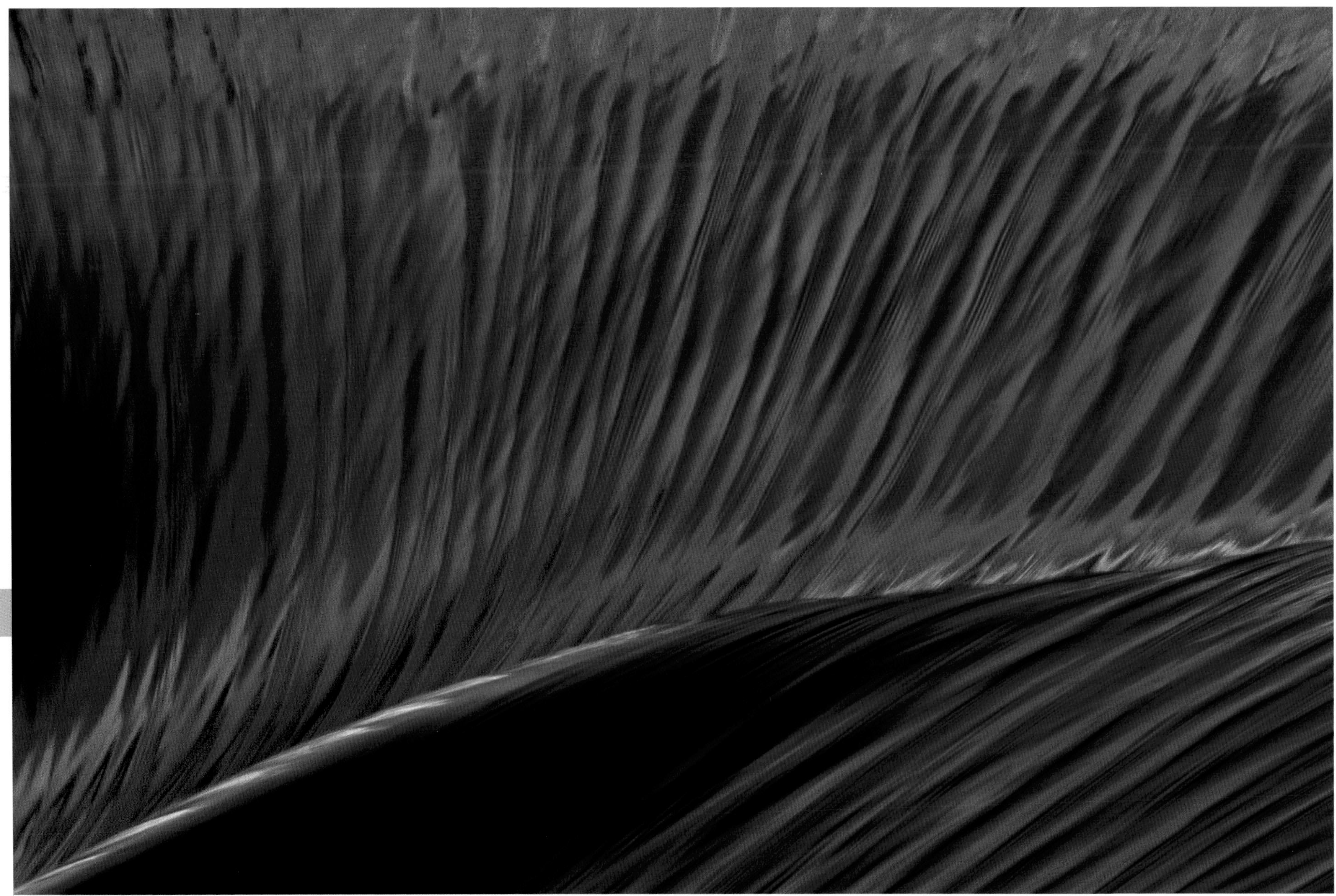

The first drop into the Rainbow Falls gorge from Whitesand Lake.

The landscape surrounding the White Gravel, White Spruce, North Swallow and Swallow rivers is extraordinarily grand. In places, we can see their volcanic origins, where fault valleys cut across the land. On the shoreline, layers of volcanic ash create mosaics of beautiful patterns, colours and textures. Black basalt ribbons and stringy white veins of quartz weave through the pink and white granite. Above the stormline we discover Pukaskwa pits dug into the beaches. These pits were used by the Anishnabe for hunting caribou, food storage and vision questing.

The rolling surf on Lake Superior resembles an ocean more than waves on a lake.

The wind-twisted pine of the North Channel was a favourite subject for Canada's famous Group of Seven painters.

Wild irises, also known as blue flags, flower in profusion on the Sleeping Giant's lowland bogs.

Time for a break and a cool swim near Gids Harbour on the Pukaskwa coast.

Gord Lake campsite, Algoma highlands.

When a cumulonimbus cloud can't rise any higher, its top spreads out into the shape of an anvil, blown in the direction of the winds at its level.

On our summer circumnavigation of Lake Nipigon, bald eagles are a common sight. Ontario's Endangered Species Act protects the bald eagle and their habitat. The adult bird, with its brown body and white head neck and tail, is easy to identify.

A cathedral grove of giant red pine greet us as we complete the 3.5-kilometre (2.2-mile) portage into Sunnywater Lake from Gamble Lake in the Lady Evelyn-Smoothwater Wilderness.

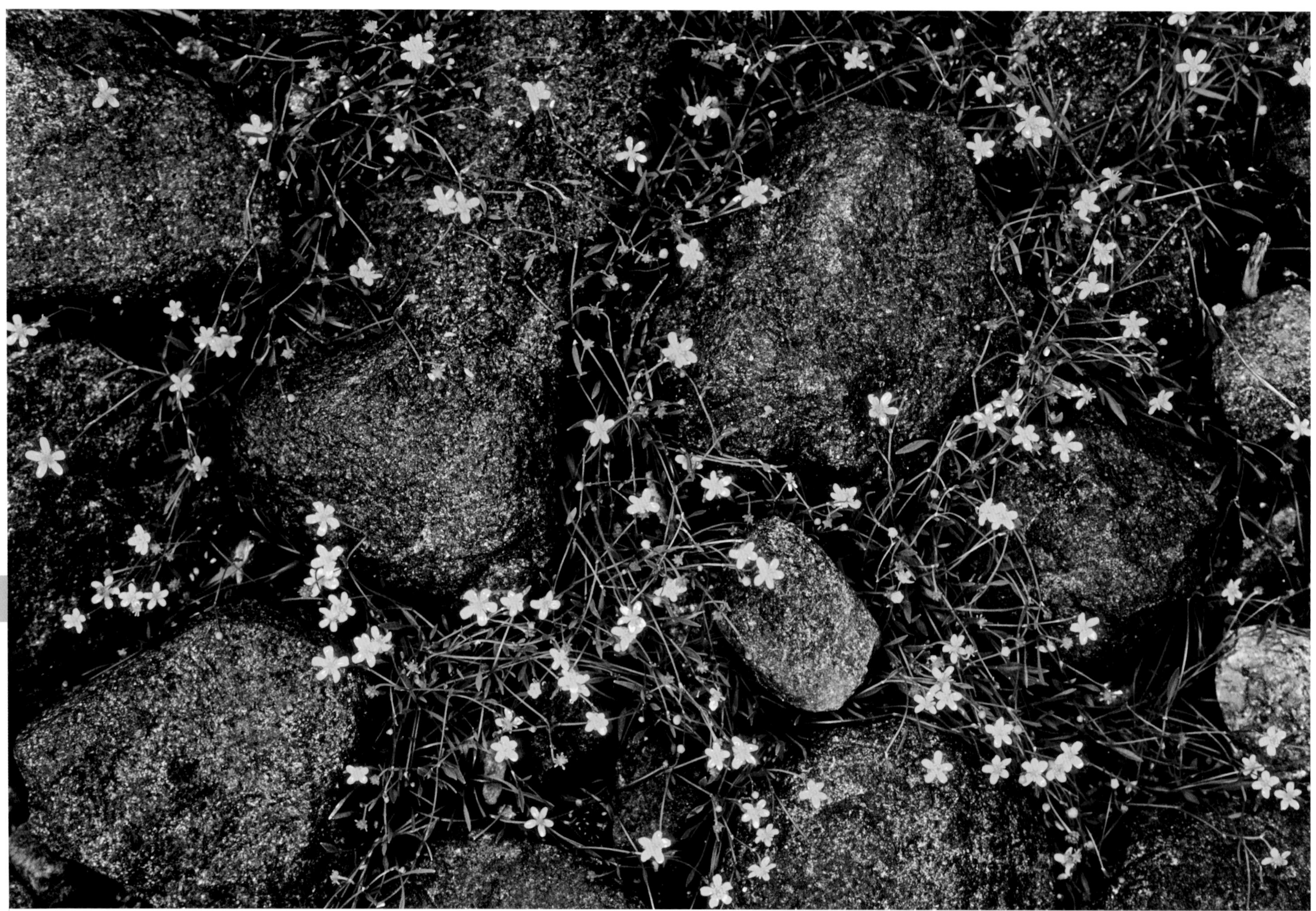

One afternoon as we paddle into a shaded cove on Lake Nipigon's north shore, we are struck by the exquisite pattern of tiny, yellow spearwort buttercups woven into the dark granite boulders at the water's edge.

Ancient headlands, sheer cliffs and bald summits characterize the coast at this spot near Oiseau Bay.

Whitewater canoeing on the Gull River.

Sunrise at Ottertail Creek, Ottawa Valley.

Autumn on Georgian Bay.

When the great fire of 1998 swept up the eastern side of Lake Nipigon, burning all but a few isolated patches of forest in its path, springtime seemed bleak on a black and smoking land. Yet five short years later when we paddle this same shoreline, we see new life everywhere: blueberries, Jack pine seedlings and fireweed in profusion.

Georgian Bay pine: a typical grouping of seven windblown white pine shows the direction of the prevailing wind in the water and in the branches.

Our favourite kind of paddling is a day when we just meander along the shore, stopping frequently to explore the nooks and crannies of the Great Lakes shoreline.

Sunset in the North Channel of Lake Huron.

Sunrise in the Benjamin Islands. North Channel of Lake Huron, west of La Cloche Mountains.

Water flowing through the forest connects one river to another, to the ocean and the clouds and the bodies of all living things. Amable du Fond River.

This image of two wolves at play, depicting some of the intimacies of the pack, was only possible to capture with the use of an infra-red remote device that triggered the shutter on the camera, as we observed their behaviour some distance away using binoculars.

Swimming in Darkwater Creek to cool off at the end of a long portage.

The Precambrian Shield of Georgian Bay's Thirty Thousand Islands, scoured clean by the glaciers, forms a multitude of low islands and shoals that actually number three times thirty thousand. Even when the mare's tails streak the sky and pine boughs sway, there are plenty of routes protected from the wind.

Early one morning on the North Peninsula of Lake Nipigon, a handsome bull moose saunters down the beach to investigate us more carefully.

Early morning fog at the south end of McAree Lake in Quetico Provincial Park.

Wave-sculpted rocks at Marathon.

Ishpatina Ridge, highest point in Ontario.

It is humbling to note that, in this century, most people on Earth will never experience a day in their lives when they are more than several yards from another human being. Out here on Lake Huron, we have set our tent near the water's edge on sun-warmed rocks, and by lantern light we cook supper. Later, we use the beam of a red flashlight to draw lines between the stars and show our daughter the constellations in the night sky. Georgian Bay.

Flocks of white pelicans are to be seen on every bay at the north end of Lake Nipigon. These gregarious water birds have been persecuted due to the misconception that they eat economically valuable species of fish. Studies have shown that these birds eat mainly fish of low economic value, such as perch, suckers, stickleback minnows and crayfish.

Low water in late summer reveals the rock structure beneath the Dog River's Denison Falls.

One thing we do frequently while paddling with friends along a shoreline indented with many coves is to play hide-and-seek. If the water is high enough you can sneak into places like this one that resemble a salt-water tidal pool.

Sunset at Fairey Island, Lake Nipigon.

Orange lichen, ox-eye daisies and purple harebells form a windblown, wave-tossed, wild garden on Moffat Strait between St. Ignace and Simpson islands.

Weathered volcanic rock on the shore of Lake Nipigon resembles the back of a giant turtle emerging from the water.

At the time the seeds for these white pine were germinating along the Sturgeon River, the earliest European explorers were venturing westward to the upper Great Lakes.

Tanner Lake, on Quetico's Dawson Trail, is part of a northeast to southwest route travelled by First Nations people for thousands of years, and later it was part of the main fur-trading route between Montreal and Lake Athabasca. The lake is named after John Tanner, a proud, intelligent man of the early 1800s, who was caught between the white culture into which he was born and the First Nations culture in which he was raised.

Storm at False Dog Harbour.

The tranquility of solo canoe travel on the shores of Lake Superior near Montreal River Harbour.

With overwhelming support from the local people, the provincial and federal governments are designating this area of 10,000 square kilometres (3,860 square miles) around Lake Superior's Rossport Islands as Canada's fourth national marine conservation area.

Sunset near Poplar Point on Lake Nipigon. Since the last ice age, people have been living in and travelling through this hub that links the Hudson Bay watershed with Lake Superior.

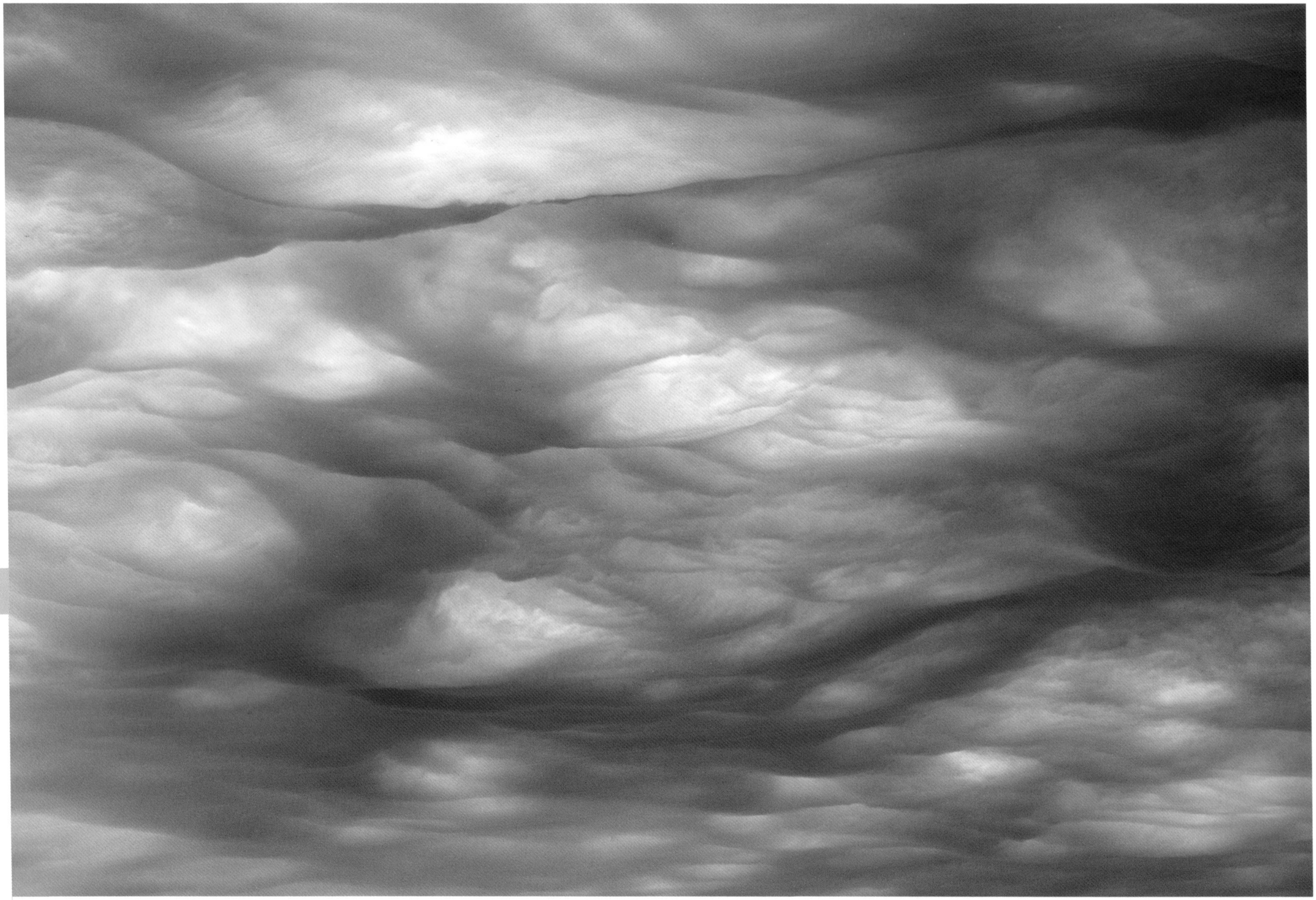

Mamma clouds hang like giant udders from the base of cumulonimbus clouds, foretelling of strong winds and heavy rain to come.

Lake Nipigon is the thirty-eighth largest lake in the world and the largest headwater to the Great Lakes–St. Lawrence waterway system.

FACING PAGE: The wild north shore of Lake Superior is a paddler's paradise. A formidable, monolithic coast for seagoing ships becomes intimate for the kayak, which can be taken off the water almost anywhere. Islands and bays screen the winds when one is in the lee, such as this particular afternoon when we duck into the deep bay on Quarry Island's east side.

RIGHT: We were very fortunate to make a calm crossing from Pie Island to Thunder Cape, a distance of 12 kilometres (7.5 miles). Here we are approaching the foot of the Sleeping Giant's cliffs.

Sunset illuminates the orange lichen on Spar Island as we admire the view to the north and west of the flat-topped mound of Pie Island and Mount McKay of the Nor'Westers, ancient home of the thunderbirds.

Floating Heart Bay at sunset.

As we paddle out of Small Lake Harbour heading east around Wilson Island, we are barely two weeks into our three-month Great Lakes Heritage Coast voyage from western Lake Superior to the southern end of Georgian Bay. Our companions are our 11-year-old Alaskan Malamut, Kalija, who travelled behind the bow seat, and our three-year-old daughter, Sila, who is in the extreme bow of the canoe.

From Foster Island, the view northeast is of the rounded hills of the Coldwell Peninsula, a scene unchanged since Dr. John Bigsby and David Thompson described it almost two hundred years ago.

Heading northeast into Ranger Bay on Basswood Lake on the second day of a 12-day, self-contained, winter traverse of Quetico Provincial Park. We travelled in the traditional manner, by snowshoe, pulling 10-foot toboggans and camping in a canvas-wall tent with a lightweight wood stove for heat.

One of the most intriguing aspects of travel by snowshoe or ski has been discovering birds and animals that neither migrate nor hibernate. More often than not their presence is revealed only by stories in the snow: crisscrossing tracks, blood and feathers, fur tufts and scat. With the aid of our camera's infrared remote device, we acquire a closer look at timber wolves, a mammal whose life story offers humans much to learn from and repect.

A rainy day is a perfect time for a walk in the boreal woods. The lichens and mosses are so fresh and green. Coloured fungi push through the leaf mould, and bumpy-backed toads that we have never seen before appear. Globally, the boreal forest is the largest terrestrial ecosystem on Earth; a third of it is within Canada, and a good bit of that in Ontario alone. This little toad is part of a complex system of trees, herbs, mosses, micro-organisms, insects and animals, all interacting among themselves and with the rock, soil, water and air.

Twin Harbours in Schreiber Channel's Collingwood Bay.

We drift in quietly toward a cow moose and her twin calves wading across a shallow bay in Lake Superior Provincial Park. The mother stops to feed on aquatic plants while the calves, ears pricked, watch us cautiously near the cover of shore.

There is nothing quite like a canoe trip through an ancient forest where the primal sounds of nature prevail. The warm wind singing through the pines, the splash of water against rock, and the clear whistle of the white-throated sparrow are some of the sounds to be heard on Haentschel Lake. These ever-changing songs mark the seasons, the time of day, the weather, and make a long-lasting impression on any traveller that may pass this way.

South of the Baldhead River in Lake Superior Provincial Park, there is a small peninsula of granite rock jutting out from a protected, sandy isthmus. It is a perfect campsite for sunset watching, camping and rock hunting.

The tranquility of solo canoe travel on the shores of Lake Superior, where one can find a place to camp even in the most unlikely of places.

A moose jaw revealed beneath the surface of Lake Nipigon sets our imaginations running with a story of what this animal's life might have been like: where it was born, how long it lived, where it travelled and how it died.

Tannins in the water, which have leached from the acidic soil, stain the Cascade River a black-tea brown.

LEFT: The graceful pink spires of fireweed, whose seeds initiate nature's renewal, are set against a backdrop of charred pine.

FACING PAGE: The size of this bonsai-like cedar, growing on a rock face at the south end of Lake Nipigon, belies the fact that it is hundreds of years old.

During a windbound day on Lake Nipigon, we "weather-watch," enjoying the ever-changing sky.

An early morning solo paddle beneath the ancient pines of the Algoma highlands.

Early morning mist on Lake Nipigon's Wabinosh Bay, after a storm chased us into its shelter the night before. Sila, Joanie and I spend most of a summer paddling the circumference of Lake Nipigon, which is the largest lake contained entirely within Ontario's boundaries and one of the largest freshwater lakes in the world.

North of Wakimika Lake, we paddle through a late afternoon rain shower that settles into a distant haze over the majestic ancient forest landscape.

The rising sun's warmth is welcome on this frosty morning canoeing on Megisan Lake in the Algoma highlands.

Heading out along 180 kilometres (110 miles) of remote coast from the Michipicoten River to the Pic River. The distant point marks the mouth of the Dog River, where we always stop to spend a day hiking up to Denison Falls.

Along with nine companions, we paddle a 36-foot replica *canot du maître* from Rossport to Red Rock. While taking a short break at the entrance to the Nipigon Channel, we imagine ourselves among a brigade of canoes passing this point during the era of the fur trade. For more than two hundred years, canoes such as these, laden with bundles of beaver pelts, traversed the north shore of Lake Superior on their way to Montreal.

From here at the edge of the highest vertical cliffs in Ontario, looking out across Thunder Bay to Pie Island, the distance appears a lot further than it did as we were making the crossing in our canoe only one day before.

View from the top of Centre Falls on Temagami's Lady Evelyn River.

A strong north wind rolling down Obabika Lake tumbles pebbles at the shore edge, making a beautiful music that is always around us in nature, if we would hush ourselves and listen. This richly complex orchestra, tuned perfectly, resonates with the billions of unique songs that describe every landscape on Earth.

A pool of water lying in a smooth rock depression on Black Bay, Georgian Bay, gives the appearance of an arch.

Two silhouettes emerge in the last light at McGregor Bay, Lake Superior Provincial Park: the giant beaver rock and the peaceful warrior.

Expedition

As the calm of the evening settles over Floating Heart Bay, a pool mirrors the sky, turning it upside down. As we reflect upon the day's travels, we notice an otter has left the story of its passing in the sand we are now camped on. In seeking out these magic places where only the sound of water, wind, and all things wild can be heard, seen and felt, we discover ourselves.

Acknowledgments

The "environment" is no further away than our next breath, and so it is odd that we toss the word around like a political football, wondering whose responsibility it is to look after "it." "It" is nothing less than ourselves and the intrinsic link we have with every living thing. Curbing our desires and improving our habits so that we consume less and experience more means a healthier, more fulfilling life. Eat local food, drink local water, buy locally made products and things that are made to last to pass on to the next generation. Taking action is within the realm of possibility for us all if we love ourselves, our children, and wish a future for our species.

The following organizations, with whom we have personal involvement, are only several of many whose work helps us to think globally and act locally to protect Wilderness Ontario:

Lake Superior Conservancy and Watershed Council
Ontario Land Trust Alliance
The Nature Conservancy of Canada
World Wildlife Fund Canada
Ontario Nature, The Federation of Ontario Naturalists
The Wildlands League,
  A Chapter of the Canadian Parks and Wilderness Society
Citizens Concerned for Michipicoten Bay
Canadian Boreal Initiative
Boreal Songbird Initiative
Northwatch

We are very grateful to the following companies for supporting us through the years in various ways to undertake wilderness journeys in Ontario and beyond. (There are many more individuals than we have space to mention. We thank you all.)

Aquabound Paddles (Joe Matuska)
Blue River Trading (Bud Shirley)
  Smart Wool
  Clif Bar
  Alpine Aire
Canon Canada
Chota Outdoor Gear (Frank Bryant)
Cooke Custom Sewing (Dan Cooke)
Confluence Watersports (Buff Grubb)
  Mad River Canoe
  Wilderness Systems
  Harmony
DayMen Photo Marketing (Uwe Mummenhoff, Michael Mayzel)
  Lowe Pro
  SanDisk
  Digipower
Fuji Photo Film Canada (Tim Berry)
Grey Owl Paddles (Brian Dorfman)
Kokatat Watersports Wear (Steve O'Meara)
Lucidia, Integrated Communications (www.garyandjoaniemcguffin.com)
Mobile Satellite Ventures (Austin Comerton)
Mountain Hardwear (Dana Nelson)
North Water Paddlesports Equipment (Lindsay Merchant)
Ostrom Outdoors (Bill and Anne Ostrom)
Raven Productions (Ms. Johnnie Hyde)
Shadow River Boatworks (Skipper Izon)
Souris River Canoes (Keith & Arlene Robinson)
Stan C. Reade Photo (James Cowie)
Subspace Communications (Dave (Smitty) Smith)
Tilley Endurables (Alex Tilley)

We are very grateful to the following friends and family for encouragement, enthusiasm, love and laughter: Irene Alexander, Vivian & Tim Alexander, Candy Beaulieu, Steve Bruno, Joe & Mary Calleri, Nancy Chapman & Bob Hansen, Mary Jo Cullen & Torfinn Hansen, Brian & Janice Christie, Ted Curry, June & Gerry Demers, Wayne & Ida Docking, Guy Dumas, Jeff Elgie, John Hieftje, Jim Hilsinger, Donna Hilsinger, Doris & Richard Kargl, Ruth O'Gawa, Jane & Paul Pellerin, Enn Poldmaa & Robin MacIntyre, Dan & Loretta Sweezey, Dave Wells, John and Jennifer Wood (Mom & Dad), and Ken & Rilla Zak.

And to our friends John Denison, Noel Hudson and Gillian Stead at Boston Mills Press who, with patience, humour and perseverance, have made this book possible!